21st Century
Junior Library

INFOGRAPHICS:
THE STOCK MARKET

Econo-Graphics Jr.

Christina Hill

T0001973

Published in the United States of America by

Cherry Lake Publishing Group
Ann Arbor, Michigan
www.cherrylakepublishing.com

Reading Adviser: Beth Walker Gambro, MS, Ed., Reading Consultant, Yorkville, IL

Photo Credits: Cover: ©Irina_Strelnikova/Getty Images; Page 1: ©Irina_Strelnikova/Getty Images; Page 7: ©Alphabet Inc/Wikimedia, ©Amazon Inc./Wikimedia, ©AT&T Corporation/Wikimedia, ©Bank of America/Wikimedia, ©Berkshire Hathaway Inc/Wikimedia, ©Chevron Corp./Wikimedia, ©Exxon Mobil/Wikimedia, ©Facebook/Wikimedia, ©McDonald's/Wikimedia, ©Microsoft Corporation/Wikimedia, ©Netflix/Wikimedia, ©OpenClipart-Vectors/Pixabay, ©Rob Janoff/Wikimedia, ©Samsung/Wikimedia, ©Tencent/Wikimedia, ©Tesla Motors/Wikimedia, ©Unknown/Wikimedia, ©VISA/Wikimedia, ©Walmart/Wikimedia, ©Wells Fargo Bank/Wikimedia; Page 8: ©Brandon Laufenberg, ©Divyansh Kumar/Pixabay, ©OpenClipart-Vectors/Pixabay; Page 9: ©DavidRockDesign/Pixabay, ©Dorigo/Pixabay, ©mauro0/Pixabay, ©mauro0/Pixabay, ©Mohamed Hassan/Pixabay, ©Unknown/Wikimedia; Page 12: ©PrathanChorruangsak/Getty Images, ©Tim Boyle/Getty Images; Page 15: ©DavidZydd/Pixabay, ©Por/Getty Images; Page 16: ©Pacific & Atlantic Photos, Inc./Library of Congress; Page 21: ©LanaStock/Getty Images

Copyright © 2023 by Cherry Lake Publishing Group

All rights reserved. No part of this book may be reproduced or utilized in any form or by any means without written permission from the publisher.

Cherry Lake Press is an imprint of Cherry Lake Publishing Group.

Library of Congress Cataloging-in-Publication Data
Names: Hill, Christina, author.
Title: Infographics. The stock market / Christina Hill.
Other titles: Stock market
Description: Ann Arbor, Michigan : Cherry Lake Publishing, [2023] | Series: Econo-graphics Jr. | Includes bibliographical references and index. | Audience: Grades 2-3 | Summary: "Why is the stock market important? In the Econo-Graphics Jr. series, young readers will examine economy-related issues from many angles, all portrayed through visual elements. Income, budgeting, investing, supply and demand, global markets, inflation, and more are covered. Each book highlights pandemic-era impacts as well. Created with developing readers in mind, charts, graphs, maps, and infographics provide key content in an engaging and accessible way. Books include an activity, glossary, index, suggested reading and websites, and a bibliography"– Provided by publisher.
Identifiers: LCCN 2022037962 | ISBN 9781668919286 (hardcover) | ISBN 9781668920305 (paperback) | ISBN 9781668921630 (ebook) | ISBN 9781668922965 (pdf)
Subjects: LCSH: Stock exchanges–United States–Juvenile literature. | Stock exchanges–Juvenile literature.
Classification: LCC HG4910 .H53 2023 | DDC 332.64/273–dc23/eng/20220824
LC record available at https://lccn.loc.gov/2022037962
Cherry Lake Publishing Group would like to acknowledge the work of the Partnership for 21st Century Learning, a network of Battelle for Kids. Please visit http://www.battelleforkids.org/networks/p21 for more information.

Printed in the United States of America
Corporate Graphics

Before embracing a career as an author, **Christina Hill** received a bachelor's degree in English from the University of California, Irvine, and a graduate degree in literature from California State University, Long Beach. When she is not writing about various subjects from sports to economics, Christina can be found hiking, mastering yoga handstands, or curled up with a classic novel. Christina lives in sunny Southern California with her husband, two sons, and beloved dog, Pepper Riley.

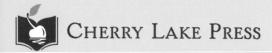

CONTENTS

WHAT IS THE STOCK MARKET?

The stock market is the buying and selling of **stocks**. A stock isn't a service. It isn't something you can see or hold. When a company needs money, it sells **shares**. They give people ownership of a piece of the company.

People who buy and sell stocks are called **investors**. Companies want to sell their stocks at a high price. But investors want to buy at a low price. **Brokers** talk to both. They settle on a price that makes both happy.

How the Stock Market Works

A company needs money. It lists its stocks on a **stock exchange**.

Investors buy stock in the company.

Brokers work to agree on a price. To start, shares must have a price of at least $4. This will get them listed on the exchange. After that, they must trade for at least $1. But many sell for thousands of dollars!

The investor now owns a share in the company. The company gets the money it needs to keep going or even grow.

THE HISTORY OF THE STOCK MARKET

In the 1300s, moneylenders met in marketplaces in Europe. They traded **loans**. They received a paper note. This legal promise said they would pay back the loan.

In 1602, the Dutch East India Company (VOC) sold shares. It was the first company to sell shares to the public.

The Value of VOC

$7.9 trillion

=

$7.9 trillion

Fast Facts

- The Dutch East India Company had 70,000 workers around the world.

- It had more than 150 ships.

- Company ships made 5,000 voyages between 1602 and 1796.

History of Wall Street

Wall Street covers eight blocks of Manhattan in New York City. It is home to the **New York Stock Exchange** (NYSE).

The NYSE building is on the corner of Broad and Wall Streets. It is a **National Historic Landmark**.

In 1792, **24 brokers** signed the Buttonwood Agreement to start the NYSE. They held meetings under a **buttonwood tree** on Wall Street.

Trading begins every morning at **9:30 a.m.** eastern standard time (EST). The **opening bell rings** at that time.

The NYSE is the largest stock exchange in the world. The total value of its stocks was **$28.4 trillion** in 2021.

What Does a Trillion Dollars Look Like?

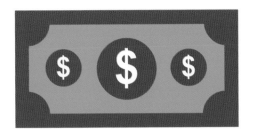

If you spent **$1 per second**, it would take you **31,700 years** to spend $1 trillion.

Laid flat, **$28.4 trillion** in $1 bills would completely cover the state of Nevada.

One trillion $1 bills laid end to end would reach from **Earth to the Sun**. The New York Stock Exchange is valued at $28.4 trillion. That's more than **14 Earth–Sun round trips**.

MEET CHARLES DOW

- Charles Dow created the Dow Jones Industrial Average in 1896.

- Dow took the average of stock prices from companies over time.

- Averages help investors see if the market is going up or down. This helps them make better choices.

2009, CNBC; 2022, Britannica

THE MODERN STOCK MARKET

It once took days to buy and sell stocks. Investors met in person with brokers. Stocks were printed on paper. They were mailed to investors.

Buying and selling stocks is much different now. This is thanks to computers and the internet. Investors can invest in companies around the world with the click of a button. More people can trade stocks.

Global Stock Exchanges

New York Stock Exchange (NYSE)	United States of America	$28.24 trillion
National Association of Securities Dealers Automated Quotations (NASDAQ)	United States of America	$24.07 trillion
Shanghai Stock Exchange	China	$7.77 trillion
Euronext	Europe	$7.38 trillion
Japan Exchange Group	Japan	$6.68 trillion
Hong Kong Exchanges	Hong Kong	$5.82 trillion
Shenzhen Stock Exchange	China	$5.76 trillion
LSE Group	United Kingdom	$3.8 trillion
National Stock Exchange of India	India	$3.43 trillion
TMX Group	Canada	$3.32 trillion

2021, Statista

Stockbrokers

THEN

- Brokers worked in person on the stock exchange floor.

- Trading licenses were required.

- Brokers made deals by shouting and motioning across the room.

NOW

- Investors buy stocks from at-home computers.

- This can take place in as little as 0.03 seconds.

- No face-to-face dealing is needed.

Top Five Most Valuable U.S. Companies in 2021

This graph is based on the value of each company's stocks.

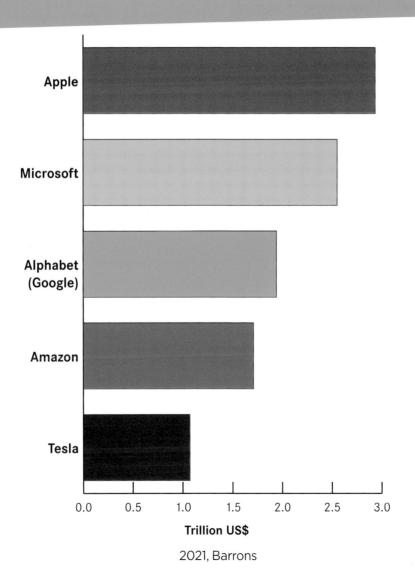

Trillion US$

2021, Barrons

STOCK MARKET CRASHES

The stock market can be risky. A popular stock is in **demand**. The price of the stock will go up. If it isn't in demand, the price can go down. A stock that sells for $100 one day could sell for $150 the next. Or it could drop to $75. There is no way to know for sure.

Bear or Bull Market?

Bear Market

- Stock prices go down.
- Investors are unsure about the stock market.
- Economy is weak.

Bull Market

- Stock prices go up.
- Investors are confident in the stock market.
- Economy is strong.

Timeline of Stock Market Crashes

The stock market goes up and down every day. But a few times, prices dropped sharply. This is called a crash.

| 1929 | Stock prices rose to record highs. But prices begin to go down in October. Investors panic and try to sell their stocks. Stock prices continue to go down for years. The **Great Depression** starts. By summer 1932, the market is down 89%. |

1920   1940   1960

A crowd gathers outside the New York Stock Exchange in 1929.

1987   Black Monday happens on October 19. The Dow stock average drops 22% in 1 day.

2000   Internet "dot-com" company stocks grow through the late 1990s. But they crash in 2000. Investors believed all dot-coms would be successful. They were wrong.

1980   **2000**   **2020**

2008   When someone asks for a loan for a house, they need to make a **down payment**. Before 2008, many home loans were offered to new buyers. These loans had very low down payments. This is risky. It causes the housing market to crash. The stock market follows.

2020   Uncertainty from the COVID-19 pandemic causes stock prices to crash. This is called the coronavirus crash.

THE FUTURE OF STOCKS

The way stocks are bought and sold has changed over time. It will likely continue to change with new technology. A new type of money is called **cryptocurrency**. It isn't a paper bill, coin, or stock. Instead, it's a digital token. People can use these tokens to buy and trade online.

Cryptocurrency vs. Stocks

Cryptocurrency

Does not represent a piece of a company

Not much history or stability

High risk

Fewer fees

Both

Used to trade

Can gain wealth or lose it by investing

Stocks

Represent a piece of a company

Long history and more stability

Less risk

More fees

AAPL • NASDAQ
Apple, Inc. **$173.07**

⬆ 0.51%
+0.88 Today

2022, NASDAQ

This is the price of one share of Apple stock at the close of the day on January 14, 2022.

The price rose 0.51% from the day before.

The price per share went up $0.88 from the opening to closing of the market.

Learning how to read stock market tables can help people become smarter investors.

ACTIVITY
Invest in the Stock Market

Now you are an expert on the stock market! You are ready to "buy" some stock! Pick three companies you would like to invest in. Think of companies you know and want to support. These could include your favorite restaurant or video game company.

1. Pretend to purchase one share of each company. Follow their stock listings for one week. You can find listings in an online newspaper or on a reliable stock website. One example is Yahoo Finance online.

2. Create a table to track your data. Check and record the price of your stocks at least once each day.

3. At the end of the week, figure out how much money you made or lost. Record the results in your table.

For a bigger challenge, give yourself a $1,000 budget to start. Try to make a profit by the end of 1 week!

LEARN MORE

Books

Cribb, Joe. *Eyewitness Money*. New York: DK Publishing, 2016.

Redling, Dylin, and Allison Tom. *Investing for Kids: How to Save, Invest, and Grow Money*. Emeryville, CA: Rockridge Press, 2020.

Websites

Britannica Kids: Stock Exchange
https://kids.britannica.com/kids/article/stock-exchange/353812

Ducksters: Money and Finance: Economics
www.ducksters.com/money/economics.php

Kiddle: Stock Exchange Facts for Kids
https://kids.kiddle.co/Stock_exchange

Bibliography

DiLallo, Matthew. "*The Biggest Stock Market Crashes in History*." The Motley Fool. Last modified June 8, 2022 https://www.fool.com/investing/stock-market/basics/crashes

The Editors of Encyclopedia Britannica. "*Stock Market Crash of 1929*." Encyclopedia Britannica. Last modified October 8, 2021. https://www.britannica.com/event/stock-market-crash-of-1929

"*The History of 'Bull' and 'Bear' Markets*." Merriam-Webster. Accessed January 10, 2022. https://www.merriam-webster.com/words-at-play/the-origins-of-the-bear-and-bull-in-the-stock-market

GLOSSARY

averages (AV-vrij-ez) values calculated by adding numbers together and then dividing the total by the number of quantities

brokers (BROH-kuhrz) people who help other people buy and sell stocks

cryptocurrency (krip-toh-KUHR-uhn-see) form of currency that exists digitally

down payment (DOWN PAY-muhnt) amount of money required to get a house loan

demand (dih-MAND) the desire to purchase goods and services

Great Depression (GRAYT dih-PREH-shuhn) the biggest economic slump in modern history starting in 1929

investors (in-VEH-stuhrz) people who use money to earn more money

loans (LOHNZ) amounts of money given in exchange for a promise of repayment

shares (SHAYRZ) units of ownership of a company

stock exchange (STAHK iks-CHAYNJ) system or place where shares of companies are bought and sold

stocks (STAHKS) value of a company that can be bought, sold, or traded as an investment

INDEX